Pringle

by Iain Gray

D1633070

Lang**Syne**

PUBLISHING

WRITING *to* REMEMBER

Lang**Syne**

PUBLISHING

WRITING *to* REMEMBER

Vineyard Business Centre,
Pathhead, Midlothian EH37 5XP
Tel: 01875 321 203 Fax: 01875 321 233
E-mail: info@lang-syne.co.uk
www.langsyneshop.co.uk

Design by Dorothy Meikle
Printed by Ricoh Print Scotland
© Lang Syne Publishers Ltd 2009

ISBN 978-1-85217-231-2

Pringle

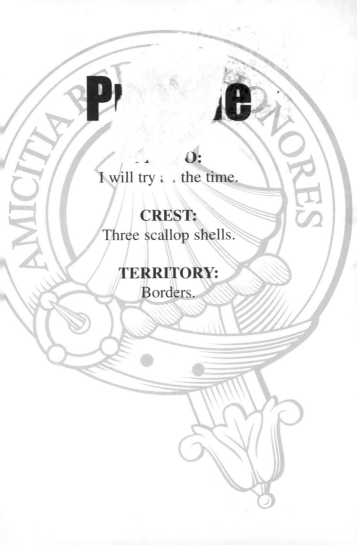

MOTTO:
I will try all the time.

CREST:
Three scallop shells.

TERRITORY:
Borders.

Chapter one:

Origins of Scottish surnames

by George Forbes

It all began with the Normans.

For it was they who introduced surnames into common usage more than a thousand years ago, initially based on the title of their estates, local villages and chateaux in France to distinguish and identify these landholdings, usually acquired at the point of a bloodstained sword.

Such grand descriptions also helped enhance the prestige of these arrogant warlords and generally glorify their lofty positions high above the humble serfs slaving away below in the pecking order who only had single names, often with Biblical connotations as in Pierre and Jacques.

The only descriptive distinctions

among this peasantry concerned their occupations, like Pierre the swineherd or Jacques the ferryman.

The Normans themselves were originally Vikings (or Northmen) who raided, colonised and eventually settled down around the French coastline.

They had sailed up the Seine in their longboats in 900AD under their ferocious leader Rollo and ruled the roost in north east France before sailing over to conquer England, bringing their relatively new tradition of having surnames with them.

It took another hundred years for the Normans to percolate northwards and surnames did not begin to appear in Scotland until the thirteenth century.

These adventurous knights brought an aura of chivalry with them and it was said no damsel of any distinction would marry a man unless he had at least two names.

The family names included that of Scotland's great hero Robert De Brus and his compatriots were warriors from families like the De Morevils, De Umphravils, De Berkelais, De Quincis, De Viponts and De Vaux.

As the knights settled the boundaries of their vast estates, they took territorial names, as in Hamilton, Moray, Crawford, Cunningham, Dunbar, Ross, Wemyss, Dundas, Galloway, Renfrew, Greenhill, Hazelwood, Sandylands and Church-hill.

Other names, though not with any obvious geographical or topographical features, nevertheless derived from ancient parishes like Douglas, Forbes, Dalyell and Guthrie.

Other surnames were coined in connection with occupations, castles or legendary deeds. Stuart originated in the word steward, a prestigious post which was an integral part of any large medieval household. The same applied to Cooks, Chamberlains, Constables and Porters.

Borders towns and forts - needed in

areas like the Debateable Lands which were constantly fought over by feuding local families - had their own distinctive names; and it was often from them that the resident groups took their communal titles, as in the Grahams of Annandale, the Elliots and Armstrongs of the East Marches, the Scotts and Kerrs of Teviotdale and Eskdale.

Even physical attributes crept into surnames, as in Small, Little and More (the latter being 'beg' in Gaelic), Long or Lang, Stark, Stout, Strong or Strang and even Jolly.

Mieklejohns would have had the strength of several men, while Littlejohn was named after the legendary sidekick of Robin Hood.

Colours got into the act with Black, White, Grey, Brown and Green (Red developed into Reid, Ruddy or Ruddiman). Blue was rare and nobody ever wanted to be associated with yellow.

Pompous worthies took the name Wiseman, Goodman and Goodall.

Words intimating the sons of leading figures were soon affiliated into the language as in Johnson, Adamson, Richardson and Thomson, while the Norman equivalent of Fitz (from the French-Latin 'filius' meaning 'son') cropped up in Fitzmaurice and Fitzgerald.

The prefix 'Mac' was 'son of' in Gaelic and clans often originated with occupations - as in MacNab being sons of the Abbot, MacPherson and MacVicar being sons of the minister and MacIntosh being sons of the chief.

The church's influence could be found in the names Kirk, Clerk, Clarke, Bishop, Friar and Monk. Proctor came from a church official, Singer and Sangster from choristers, Gilchrist and Gillies from Christ's servant, Mitchell, Gilmory and Gilmour from servants of St Michael and Mary, Malcolm from a servant of Columba and Gillespie from a bishop's servant.

The rudimentary medical profession was represented by Barber (a trade which also once included dentistry and surgery) as well as Leech or Leitch.

Businessmen produced Merchants, Mercers, Monypennies, Chapmans, Sellers and Scales, while down at the old village watermill the names that cropped up included Miller, Walker and Fuller.

Other self explanatory trades included Coopers, Brands, Barkers, Tanners, Skinners, Brewsters and Brewers, Tailors, Saddlers, Wrights, Cartwrights, Smiths, Harpers, Joiners, Sawyers, Masons and Plumbers.

Even the scenery was utilised as in Craig, Moor, Hill, Glen, Wood and Forrest.

Rank, whether high or low, took its place with Laird, Barron, Knight, Tennant, Farmer, Husband, Granger, Grieve, Shepherd, Shearer and Fletcher.

The hunt and the chase supplied Hunter, Falconer, Fowler, Fox, Forrester, Archer and Spearman.

The renowned medieval historian Froissart, who eulogised about the romantic deeds of chivalry (and who condemned Scotland as being a poverty stricken wasteland), once sniffily dismissed the peasantry of his native France as the jacquerie (or the jacques-without-names) but it was these same humble folk who ended up overthrowing the arrogant aristocracy.

In the olden days, only the blueblooded knights of antiquity were entitled to full, proper names, both Christian and surnames, but with the passing of time and a more egalitarian, less feudal atmosphere, more respectful and worthy titles spread throughout the populace as a whole.

Echoes of a far distant past can still be found in most names and they can be borne with pride in commemoration of past generations who fought and toiled in some capacity or other to make our nation what it now is, for good or ill.

Chapter two:

Pilgrims' progress

**As one of the oldest surnames to be found in
the hills and valleys of the Scottish Borders, it
should come as no surprise to learn that long
generations of bearers of the name of Pringle
have been at the very heart of Scotland's
colourful and turbulent story.**

The name itself has its roots in the soil of
the Borders landscape, stemming as it does from
the Old Norse 'Hopringle', or 'Hoppringle',
meaning a circular hollow, or dell – with 'hop'
indicating a valley and 'ringle' a ring.

This 'circular hollow' is located in the
Borders parish of Stow, on the Gala Water,
about ten miles north of the town of Galashiels,
and appears to have been the original territory of
the Pringles.

From Stow, the family branched out over
succeeding centuries to other locations throughout the Borders.

Some of these important branches include the Pringles of Whitsome and Smailholm, the Pringles of Stichill, the Pringles of Soutra Aisle, the Pringles of Clifton and Haining, the Pringles of Fountainhall, the Pringles of Torsonce, the Pringles of Galashiels, and the Pringles of Earlside.

The family also acquired lands in Midlothian, while descendants of the original Border Pringles can be found today as far afield as the northeast of Scotland, Ireland, North America, and South Africa.

The chief of the family was known as Pringle of that Ilk and, following the death of the last Pringle of that Ilk in the early years of the eighteenth century, the main family became the Pringles of Stitchill.

Sir Robert Pringle, a son of the Stitchill branch, was created a baronet in 1683, and this proud title is still retained by the family.

'Pringle' became the established spelling of the name in the mid-seventeenth century, but up until that date other forms included Hopringill, Hopringle, Hoppringle, Pryngel,

Pringill, and even Obrinkel – with an Elys de Obrinkel recorded in 1296 and a Wilhelmo Hopringill, the first of the family to be known as 'of that Ilk', recorded in 1391.

One of the most prominent Pringle families was the Pringles of Soutra Aisle, once the site of a magnificent complex of buildings built by Scotland's Malcolm IV in 1164.

The famous complex comprised not only a monastery and church, but also a hospice, or hospital, known as the Hospice of Soutra, or the House of the Holy Trinity at Soutra.

Founded by the Augustinian religious order, it was operated with a care to medical techniques and an efficiency that would impress even health authorities of today.

It catered for the needs of the hundreds of footsore and weary pilgrims who travelled the pilgrim route of devotion to the famous Borders abbeys of Jedburgh, Dryburgh, Melrose, and Kelso, and also held an important status as a refuge, or sanctuary, for fugitives from the harsh justice of the times.

Located less than five miles from the Pringle territory of Stow, the hospice flourished until the late fifteenth century, while an important bridge that was on the pilgrim route was known as Pringill's Brig.

The Pringles were closely allied to the cause of Scotland's freedom during the thirteenth century War of Independence, when successive armies of English invaders laid waste to the entire Borders area.

They were early supporters of the great warrior king Robert the Bruce, who won his famous victory over the military might of England's Edward II at the battle of Bannockburn in 1314.

Sir James Pringle, of the Pringles of Whitsome, is said to have been a friend of Bruce and following the king's death, he was among the elite band of renowned Scottish knights who accompanied Sir James Douglas on a mission in 1330 to bury his heart in the Holy Land.

Attacked by Moors while travelling through Spain, Lord James was killed, but Sir nes Pringle was among those surviving knights who brought Bruce's heart back to Scotland, where it was later solemnly interred in the grounds of Melrose Abbey.

One theory, that does not stand up to close scrutiny, however, is that the name Pringle stems from 'son of the pilgrim', and that this explains the three scallop shells on the Pringle family crest and coats-of-arms.

But while the scallop shell was, indeed the 'badge' of pilgrims, a likelier explanation for the scallop shells is that they commemorate Sir James Pringle's pilgrimage to the Holy Land with the heart of Bruce, and may also even commemorate the Pringle association with the pilgrim centre at Soutra.

Intriguingly, a winged heart appeared on the crest of those knights such as Sir James Pringle who undertook the pilgrimage with Bruce's heart, and this device also appears on some of the Pringle coats of arms.

One of the Pringle family mottos, meanwhile, is 'I will try all the time.'

While there is no official Pringle tartan as such, bearers of the name traditionally wear any one of the three 'regional' Galawater tartans – Galawater, Galawater Old, and Galawater New.

The Pringles were closely allied to the Douglases, and their fate was often closely intertwined with that of this powerful and ambitious Borders family.

From an early date in the fourteenth century, the Pringles acted as 'scrutifers', or squires, to the Earls of Douglas, and Adam de Hoppringill served as squire to James, the 2nd Earl of Douglas, at the battle of Otterburn, in Northumberland, on August 5, 1388.

The Scots had earlier been involved in a skirmish outside the walls of Newcastle when the young Earl of Douglas managed to snatch the silk pennant from the lance of his adversary Henry Percy, heir to the 1st Earl of Northumberland and better known to posterity as Henry Hotspur.

Douglas proceeded to lead his army back towards Scotland, but Hotspur, stung by the insult to his honour, swore his precious pennant would never be allowed to cross the border.

He pursued Douglas, and the two armies clashed at Otterburn, the young earl receiving a fatal blow, while his squire, Adam de Hoppringill fell dead at his side.

As the Scots army faltered, demoralised over the fate of their commander, Sir James Lindsay knelt by his side and asked him how he fared, to which Douglas replied: 'dying in my armour, as my fathers have done, thank God!'

On Douglas's dying command, Lindsay raised the famed Banner of the Bloody Heart of the Douglases, rallied the Scots, and led them to victory.

In a later century, Thomas Hoppringil was James IV's principal trumpeter, and in this role he sounded the charge for what proved to be the disastrous battle of Flodden, fought on September 9, 1513, and in which he was among the 5,000 Scots including the king, an archbishop, two bishops, eleven earls, fifteen barons, and 300 knights who were killed.

The headstrong James had embarked on the venture after Queen Anne of France, under the terms of the Auld Alliance between Scotland and her nation, appealed to him to 'break a lance' on her behalf and act as her chosen knight.

Crossing the border into England at the head of a 25,000-strong army that included 7,500 clansmen and their kinsmen, James engaged a 20,000-strong force commanded by the Earl of Surrey.

Despite their numerical superiority and bravery, however, the Scots proved no match for the skilled English artillery and superior military tactics of Surrey.

From the late fourteenth century until the late fifteenth century, many of the younger daughters of some of the Pringle families served as prioresses of Coldstream Abbey.

One of the most notable of these was Isabella Hopringill, a daughter of Adam Pringle of Burnhouse Tower.

Hearing of the tragic defeat of the Scots army at Flodden, the doughty prioress immediately arranged for the corpses, many of them horribly mutilated, to be brought for burial in the consecrated grounds of the abbey.

This deed is still commemorated in a colourful and moving annual ceremony when a sod is cut from the site of the battlefield and carried back on horseback to the Tweed Green in Coldstream.

Chapter three:

Killing times

The Scottish Borders area was for many centuries a virtual byword for lawlessness, with a Privy Council report as late as 1608, for example, graphically describing how the 'wild incests, adulteries, convocation of the lieges, shooting and wearing of hackbuts, pistols, lances, daily bloodshed, oppression, and disobedience in civil matters, neither are nor has been punished.'

Many of the families were known as reivers, taking their name from the custom of reiving, or raiding, not only their neighbours' livestock, but also that of their neighbours across the border.

The word 'bereaved', for example, indicating to have suffered loss, derives from the original 'reived', meaning to have suffered loss of property.

In an attempt to bring a semblance of

order into the chaotic state of affairs on both sides of the border, Alexander II of Scotland had in 1237 signed the Treaty of York, which for the first time established the border with England as a line running from the Solway to the Tweed.

On either side of the border there were three 'marches' or areas of administration, the West, East, and Middle Marches, and a warden governed these.

Complaints from either side of the border were dealt with on Truce days, when the wardens of the different marches would act as arbitrators; there was also a law known as the Hot Trod, that granted anyone who had their livestock stolen the right to pursue the thieves and recover their property.

In the Scottish borderlands, the Homes and Swintons dominated the East March, while the Armstrongs, Maxwells, Johnstones, and Grahams were the rulers of the West March.

The Kerrs, along with the Douglases and Elliots, held sway in the Middle March.

The Pringles appear to have been one of

the few exceptions to the rather anarchic lifestyle of their neighbours, probably because they had too much to lose – flourishing contentedly on the lands they already held.

An indication of the extent of their land-holdings is found in the fact that in 1592 they are on record as having sworn an oath to serve the Wardens of both the Middle and the East Marches.

The family also became heavily involved from about the mid sixteenth century in the immensely lucrative Borders wool trade, while in 1815 Robert Pringle bought a mill in Hawick, laying the foundations for the world-renowned Pringle knitwear range.

Pringles also became involved in the destructive civil wars that raged between Crown and Covenant that followed the signing in February of 1638 of a National Covenant that pledged to uphold the Presbyterian religion.

Signed at Edinburgh's Greyfriars Church by nobles, barons, burgesses and ministers, it was subscribed to the following day by hundreds of ordinary people.

Copies were made and dispatched around Scotland and eagerly signed by thousands more, and they became known as Covenanters

The authorities mercilessly hounded these Covenanters, and many were summarily executed on the spot without trial, while others were tortured and executed or sold into servitude far from home.

Among the Covenanters' many persecutors was James Hoppringle of Buckholm Tower, whose evil deeds are said to be responsible for a ghost that is still said to haunt the ruins of the Borders tower.

During what was known as the Killing Time, from 1682 to 1685, when the persecution was particularly ruthless, he sallied forth from his fortified tower one day to indulge in his favourite pastime of hunting down fugitive Covenanters with two of his ferocious hounds.

A number of Covenanters had gathered on a moor and scattered at the approach of the laird – but two, a Geordie Elliot and his son, William, were captured and thrown into the stinking depths of the dungeon of Buckholm Tower.

One of the prisoners was in agony from wounds he had received and his cries incurred the wrath of the drunken laird, who stormed into the dungeon, slamming its heavy door behind him.

For several minutes the only sound his terrified servants heard were the sickening cries of pain and pathetic pleas for mercy – and then silence.

The laird returned to the comfort of his warm fire and brandy, and was interrupted once again when Geordie Elliot's wife, Isobel, arrived to plead for mercy for her husband and son.

Untouched by her tears, the heartless laird dragged her to the dungeon, threw open the door, and her horrified gaze was met with the sight of her husband and son hanging like slaughtered beasts from two hooks in the ceiling.

Mad with grief, Isobel Elliot is said to have cursed the laird for all eternity, and he died in torment shortly afterwards, complaining that he had been pursued by a pack of spectral hounds.

Matters did not rest there, however,

because just before the first anniversary of his mysterious death his ghostly form was seen near the tower, chased by the hounds.

This apparition was followed on successive nights by the sound of hounds baying and pathetic cries for help and, on the actual anniversary of his death, equally frightening sounds were heard from the dungeon.

On every anniversary of his death since, the dank ruins of Buckholm Tower are still said to echo with the ghostly sounds.

Chapter four:

Medical innovators

In later centuries, the Pringles displayed a diversity of talents in a number of fields, and one of the most notable of the name was Sir John Pringle, born in 1707, and the youngest son of Sir John Pringle, of Stitchell House, near Kelso.

After studying medicine and practising for a time as a doctor in Edinburgh, he was appointed in 1742 as the personal physician to the Earl of Stair, commander of the British Army in Flanders, and put in charge of the hospital there.

Later in the year he was appointed Surgeon General to the British Expeditionary Force in Silesia, in the War of the Austrian Succession.

This was an age when practically non-existent standards of hygiene led to rampant diseases such as typhus and dysentery being responsible for more deaths among troops than actual battle.

A firm believer that prevention is better than cure, it was in Flanders that Pringle enforced a strict regime of high standards of cleanliness in what then passed for military hospitals.

In June of 1743, at the time of the battle of Dettingen, in Bavaria, he sowed the seeds for what later would become the world-renowned organisation of the International Red Cross.

He was responsible for an agreement with the French commander that the military hospitals on both sides should be regarded as neutral sanctuaries for the sick and wounded and so protected by both sides – and the concept of the International Red Cross, with provisions for the care of prisoners of war, developed from this.

In 1750, two years before he married a daughter of Dr William Oliver of Bath, of 'Bath Oliver' biscuits fame, Pringle submitted three papers to the Philosophical Transactions of the Royal Society on *Experiments on Septic and Antiseptic Substances*.

A friend of the explorer Captain James Cook, he had also recognised the problem of scurvy among sailors and studied ways of preventing it.

In 1776 William Anderson, Captain Cook's surgeon, discovered a special type of cabbage on a South Atlantic island and, recognising its ability to ward off scurvy when boiled up with pork, beef, or peas, it was named after Pringle under the Latin title *Pringlea antiscorbutica*.

Pringle, who was awarded a baronetcy in 1776 and at one time held the post of physician to the king, died in 1782, and a monument to his memory was erected in Westminster Abbey.

He is also commemorated on a special frieze in the London School of Hygiene and Tropical Medicine.

Another medical innovator was James Hogarth Pringle, born in New South Wales in 1863.

He worked throughout Europe, and it was while practising at the Glasgow Royal Infirmary between 1896 and 1923 that he developed what is known today as the Pringle Manoeuvre, a surgical technique used in abdominal procedures.

Thomas Pringle, who was born in the Scottish Borders in 1789, was the accomplished poet who was both a contemporary and a friend of Sir Walter Scott.

In contemporary times, David Pringle is the respected Scottish-born science fiction editor who has edited several guides on the subject, including the best-selling *The Ultimate Guide to Science Fiction*.

On the stage, Aileen Pringle, born Aileen Bisbee in California in 1895, and who died in 1989, was a popular stage and film actress during the era of silent films. Her husband was Charles McKenzie Pringle, whose wealthy father owned estates in Jamaica.

On the high seas, Vice Admiral Joel Pringle, who was born in 1873, was a distinguished American naval officer who was awarded the Distinguished Service Medal for his service during the First World War as commanding officer of the U.S.S. Melville.

The Fletcher Class Destroyer, the U.S.S. Pringle, which saw service during the Second

World War, was named after him, while Pringle Hall, in the U.S. Naval War College, is also named in his honour.

In the world of sport, William Alvin Moody, born in Mobile, Alabama, in 1954, is better known as the famous American wrestling manager Percy Pringle.

Derek Pringle, born in Kenya in 1958, is a former English cricketer who played for Essex between the late 1970s and early 1990s.

Now a popular cricket correspondent, during his playing career he also played thirty Test Matches between 1982 and 1992, scoring a staggering 695 runs and taking 70 wickets.

Mike Pringle, although born in Los Angeles in 1967, is a former Canadian football running back who broke a number of records during his career in the Canadian Football League.

'Pringle' is also the name of a town in Custer County, South Dakota, and a borough in Luzerne County, in Pennsylvania.